Morphology

by Erica Miriam Fabri

Write Bloody Publishing

writebloody.com

First edition.
ISBN: 978-1949342666

Cover Design by Derrick C. Brown
Interior Layout by Nikki Steele
Edited by Haley Hutchinson
Proofread by Sam Rose Preminger
Author Photo by Erica Miriam Fabri

Type set in Bergamo.

Printed in the USA

Write Bloody Publishing
Los Angeles, CA

Support Independent Presses
writebloody.com

For Jacqui, who is my favorite poem.

Morphology

Morphology

morphology: (noun)

- (BIOLOGY: HUMAN)
  the study of the forms and structures of the human body.
- (LINGUISTICS)
  the study of the forms and structures of words.

DEAR POETRY,

I almost died without you.
Then, you returned to me as a house
with one hundred old doors
that moaned when they opened
and closed. I couldn't sneak in
or out, of any room,
without waking my self up
from even the darkest sleep.

Sometimes, I need to quiet my whole body
before I can be with you. Other times,
in a mid-fever moment, I grasp for you
like a cliff-fallen creature.

I know that grief conceives you.
I know heartache makes you grow.
But you feed on love. You eat fistfuls of it.
Thick hair sprouts in strange places.
Toenails rip shoes to shreds.
What a monster you can be
if you are not allowed to make
the noises you are meant to make.

Wild Thing. Your yellow eyes
do not frighten me.
They are candles.
You pointed me back to me.
I was an ocean away.

Part I
Grief is a Garden

THIS IS THE VOCABULARY LIST FOR THIS BOOK OF POETRY

Yellow
Rat
Light

Heart
Honey
Seed

Immortal
Skeleton
Swimming

Jellyfish
Moon
Animal

Golden
Rodent
Tongue

Spider-web
River
Bees

Cyclone
Sea
Stars

Shark
Wave
Electricity

Old
Tornado
Fog

THE GREATEST POEM EVER WRITTEN

The greatest poem ever written
must be a love poem. There must be
a tongue in this poem, with its own
animal heart, and two lips that suck skin
like warm dumplings.

But. The greatest poem ever written,
must also be a war poem, where people
eat grenades instead of sandwiches,
where children remember their homes
only as lightning bolts.

If I build this poem on a mountain
overlooking a dragon-shaped lake,
I cannot be afraid of falling
from the roof of the poem
to my doom. Instead, I must learn
the recipe for making a neon rainbow
that floats like a fog between old trees.

There will be ghosts. After all,
it is the greatest poem ever written,
which means people love people who die
and haunt their dark windows.
The dead return as green light-energy.
They sneak into our bodies at the feet,
then ripple through our legs
like an ocean wave.
We have sex, and we pretend
it is not the ghost in us
compassing our hips.

Because this is the greatest poem
ever written, it needs to be true.
We are already residents
of the insane asylum, a straitjacket
is the only quilt we own.
What *are* eyeballs? What *are* eyeballs? Are *you* an eyeball?

You are late to work.
You live in New York City.
Your bag is too heavy.
You are certain
today will be the day
your collar bone snaps
like a carrot
from the ferocious weight.
You are holding a paper cup of tea.
When you try to squeeze honey
into the rising steam, you miss —
the sticky golden goo
oozes over the lines
of your palm.
You can lick it off,
or you can throw yourself
into traffic.

I daydream of taking a long,
hot shower, while the whole world burns.
I stand alone in the bathtub.
Outside, tornadoes of fire roar.
Flames are arms.
Come and get me. Holy hands. Take me.

Morphology

"Scientists have made an artificial jellyfish out of a rat's heart." -NBC News

If a rat's heart can be made
into a jellyfish that can swim
as an umbrella swims with the wind,
what else can be renewed
from the sewer to the sea?

If I peel away a small part of a forearm,
not enough for anyone to notice, only
a strand the same width as spider-web silk,
can I use it to sew a citrus tree,
with fruits that swing like bells?

I will wear a dress of lemons. I will carry
all the hungry children in a bag of netting.
No one will recognize them.
I will have disguised them as lemons.

Maybe this is the only way to become immortal?
By unfolding the four chambers
of a rodent's pumping organ
until it is a flat flower-shaped noodle.
Lay it in a pool of water. Feed it blue electricity
the way you feed soup to the sick,
bring the beat back. Beat. Back.

Divorce Poem

Why does Daddy work at night,
and Mommy work in the daytime?

Because a singer's job is in the dark.
And a poet's job is in the light.

Is it because Daddy only loves the Moon,
and Mommy only loves the Sun?

Oh, no. I know Daddy loves the Sun.
And Mommy *really* loves the Moon.

Both Daddy and Mommy,
love *both* the Sun and the Moon?

They do.

THE MEDUSA OF RATS

Her hair is the color of sewer rats.
It rides her scalp like a rope ladder
of braided rodents, tied tail to tooth,
tail to tooth. The Medusa of Rats
now sleeps on the mattress
where I made my son.
The Medusa of Rats cooks (badly)
in the kitchen that my father built
with his thick hands.

Her horse's mane of rat–on–rat–chain
was cast as lead–mutant
in the nightmare I once imagined
I could not survive. But, look, I am alive.
How she saved me. Every last rat–part of her.
Her whole rat–self took my place
in a windowless world.

My new home is a greenhouse.
The fifty–three seeds I planted,
in clay pots, took root; leafy vines
stretch their arms from room
to room, weaving a blanket of jungle.

The nightmare is upside down now:
I do not fear her animal–hair
crawling up the brick wall
of my old life. I rest easy.
Her vermin keep her up at night.

Light for You

By the time we met, I had only one bone
left in my body. Turtles can't be removed
from their shells, but I had become
a gooey skin-woman and almost no one
noticed. Under an x-ray, I was mistaken
for an octopus. The doctor told me:
Your heartbeat is your calendar. I didn't
want him to photograph my inside self:
instead, I had asked him to explain why
my hands had become too heavy to carry.
They were filled to the fingertips with electricity.
I tried to be light. I tried, very hard, to be light for you.

Love Poem Redux

I have to write this poem fast,
today, tonight, before
it's gone again.
It happened right here,
in this interstellar
space, right around the time
when we all heard
what a black hole sounded like
for the first time.
It had been years, tens of thousands
of hours. I was certain
that this specific thunder
would never return to my sky;
and then, it did. Like a UFO
from the farthest star system.
It even brought back the missing moon.
A massive pendant, crowning
over the three bridges I have loved
my entire life, mighty and polished,
their iron skeletons arched
toward white light.

Then later, that stony, golden, moon-
body, affixed to my tiny architecture
of muscle and bone,
spoke to me, between kisses,
in a coded language.
I cannot write the translation
with this alphabet.
I do not dare speak it out loud
using lips. Maybe I am asleep
crafting a myth, or worse,
awake inside a hallucination,
because I have finally
unhinged my skull
like the top of a pillbox.
If so, then my madness
made this: the first Love Poem
since the cyclone uprooted me.

A New Love poem carved out
of nothing soft, nothing stormless,
because all the soft stuff
got eaten,
and all the storm
still sings.

Making Love to the Grief Body

He undresses in a flash. His gold torso
is shaped like a tombstone.
The Grief Body is fire to touch.
But my throat is home to an inside river
of spit, a reservoir of drool, that mudslides
over our shoulders, making all
of our everything, slippery.

The Grief Body, like a shark, swallows
his food whole, without chewing. I offer
my legs. I am trying to feed the fever out of him.
I am trying to prove that my hands
are leeches. That if he will let me, I can
suck out the sorrow with these wet palms.

If I were a doctor, I would tell him what science says:
that the apex of his heart has ballooned.
But since I am a poet, I ask him to do
the same thing he did last time:

peel my backbone out of its skin
and feed it to me, bone by bone,
until I have a belly-full of skeleton.
Let me make a wheel out of hips.
Let me grind the grief away.
Tear off my arms. You can have them.
They're yours now.

A Very Dirty Poem

Welcome to a very dirty poem.
Do not come inside this poem
unless you are ready for mud. This poem
will touch you with an unclean arm,
gift you horses' legs, liquify your bed.

You think you know what dirty is? You don't.
So, you had a lover, with a vacuum for a throat?
Sure, that's nice. But have you ever been transformed
from mortal to poem?

What will you do when your lungs
become cyclones? When nine
out of ten of your fingers quake?
When your eyeballs mutate into marbles?

You think you're filthy? You're not.
What? You've been inside a blimp-sized backside?
You, beast, you. But what will you do
when you are trapped in a nightmare,
drowning in an old hotel, and you cannot
make yourself wake up?

I will spit honey into your mouth
and watch you rise to the surface
of that secret sea. If you bury your hands
in me, I am garden soil, you will never die.
Dig deeper and more will grow. More will grow.

BEES

Last night, in bed, I was attacked by bees
and you slept through the whole thing.
They didn't want a single bite of you.
I can't imagine why not.
In the morning, you woke up
and examined my legs.
They were covered with stings
shaped like tiny onions.
It could have been a lot worse,
you said. And that was true.
Almost always is. You leaned down
to kiss my ankle, and I asked
if you were going to try to suck
the venom out. *No*, you said,
the poison could ruin my teeth.
Besides, it would make more sense
for me to suck out the sweet.

How Shadows are Made

I love you, but a whale of a shadow escorts you
to every door. You can't crawl out, from inside
the shadow's shell, for long enough to dig up
the dirt. I want to help you find enough yellow
to dismantle the shadow, but there are strong
storms on the sun's surface. I want you slapped
up against me, but your shadow is as unnerving
as swimming with sharks, and I have been trying
to find something in this world that feels better
than making love to you, but, instead, I am eating
rattlesnake after rattlesnake. My want is an army,
greedy as the want men have for power. But I do not
do what men do when they want. I do not tear limbs
off bodies to win land, but I do pull petals off ox-eyes,
one by one, as I ask the golden circle to tell me
if you can see me, my love, when you are submerged
in shadow; can you see me, here, in the dark place?

Fog

He carries a bucket of used bullets.
She is balancing a baking dish of broken
heart parts on her palms. Because of these
things, they cannot use their arms
to hold each other. They are both
trying to get home, except it is
a brand-new home that they are
thirsty for. He is starving. She offers
to cook the bloody organ. He needs
a place to dump the old dark stuff.
A kitchen timer rings. The shower
starts spitting water so hot
it fills the whole apartment
with steam. He cannot see her,
but he can still smell her.

She realizes the only way
to find him in this fog,
is to read a poem to him.
Just then, her tongue
falls out of her mouth
onto the floor. It flops
like a fish on land, making
slapping sounds. There is a knock
at the door. She wants to say:
Please, don't let anybody in.
But her words won't work.

THE POOL WAS EMPTY

My son and I are standing on a street corner
in Brooklyn, his arms wrap around my waist,
his face buried in the belly part of my green sundress.
He is sobbing loudly. Everyone is looking at us.
He cannot make the hard, hard, crying stop.
I can't either. Between his hyperventilating gasps
he shouts: *This is the worst day of my life!*
It isn't. But today, I don't have the energy
to convince him otherwise; the usual frustration
in my gut that moves me to lecture him
on how golden his life is compared to refugee children,
because I am also heartbroken and trying
to hold my own bones in place for a few more hours.
When he is able to manage words, he tells me
only bad things have happened today:
his friend didn't meet him at the playground,
the strap on his favorite goggles broke,
and we wanted to go swimming, but the pool
was empty. At this moment, there is nothing sadder
than an empty pool. A giant concrete hole, a blue grave,
and the ungentle way it announces that summer is over.
The hollow echo that replaces cool water.
The cruelness of everyone. No one was loving enough
just yesterday, to tell us, it was, in fact,
our last swim of the year. It feels impossible
to accept, without any warning, that our bodies
will no longer be able to do this thing
that our bodies so love to do.
I am no longer talking about swimming.
God—how we might have used our arms and legs
differently, if we had known
it was our last time together.

Part II
The Muse Moved to the Sky

First Love

I return most often to that one boiling night,
when we said goodbye through the screen door.
Our sixteen-year-old noses rubbed against the place
where flies crawl, where insects grip wire mesh, looking for
light, warmth, a way inside, or just a place to take a rest
before their next flight. The scene comes back to me like an echo:
you step away, look back, a gray filter shading your clock-face.
What if I had called you back? What if I ripped the screen
with my teeth like an animal? What could I have changed?
Does some of the rubber behind your eye sockets melt away?
Do your lungs grow fists? Let's say I swallow, every last drop
of every last thing that I siphon out of you; then what?
Do I make you brand new? The morning you died,
I hadn't slept. My infant son had spent all the dark hours
crawling on me, begging for more of me. My father called
and, when I heard his voice, I felt a tornado of rocks rising
from my middle, then I just kept saying no. No, no, no.
No, no, no. Oh no. No.

Two Kinds of Cake

After I came home from your funeral,
I baked forty-eight cupcakes
for my son's first birthday. The recipe
was strange, the ingredients
didn't blend smooth:
a heaping cup of grief folded into
freshly melted sweet joy; a ceremony
for death, mixed in the same bowl
as a revelry of birth; the hard knowing
that you will never grow older,
topped with a celebration of days
because my baby boy has.

There is no order here.
No reservations were made
to schedule when the soft parts
of me would be pulled in one direction
or another. If my Love is a kite,
two different winds are flying me
to two far-reaching parts
of the same sky.

There are No Tattoos in Heaven

Last night, you came to visit me in a dream.
You told me, there are no tattoos in heaven,
and held out your arms, wiped clean, as proof.

You asked if I wanted to know more
about what it's like to live in the sky.
I could tell you were tired by the way
your body hung itself on the chair next to me.
The clouds must have peeled twenty years
off your skin. You wore dark brown hair, like a teenager.
You came back as the version of you I loved first.
The version I loved most.

There was too much to catch up on and I didn't know
how much time we had. I told you I was having a hard time
making poems without you here. That even though I'd been
so angry with you, for so many years, I didn't want you to die.

I told you my son is a masterpiece, that every day ignites
and detonates a cannonball thing inside me. I told you
that I do not go one day without remembering you,
and wondering how you always knew, since we were kids,
that you would die so young. Why did we never believe you?

You told me, again, that there are no tattoos in heaven,
so, save your money. They are just a temporary stain.
Or, on second thought, you said: No, go ahead,
get as many tattoos as you can afford. Their full-color life
is fleeting. They decorate the flesh for such a short time.
Savor every needled line.

I begged you to stay longer. But it was an impossible request.
No one gets to tell their dreams what to do.
I asked if you still remembered the screen door,
the coconut, the handfuls of pennies, the lake. You didn't.

It was then that I realized, the dead don't recognize us.
They leave us behind, and we spend the rest of our days
twisting our limbs, making ourselves turn colors
in our attempts
to bring them back to life.

Quantum Entanglement is the Scientific Explanation for Love

A bizarre, counter-intuitive
phenomenon
that cannot be explained
by classical physics:
the idea that
if two particles
are entangled
and you separate them,
they will continue to be
intimately linked
even when billions
of light-years of space
grow between them.

You have been dead for seven years.
Does a small part of you still live under my fingernail?

The night you died,
I remember reaching into the dark for him.
A black hole slept on the pillow beside me
instead of a husband.
It had a whistle for a snore.

Was the shadow version of you
still close to Earth that night?
How fast were you able to jet
yourself into the stars? How far
have you gone? Do you measure
distance by color now? Can you see
the moon is shaped like a lemon?
Sunsets on Mars, are blue?
There is a leaf in a desert
that can never die.
A jar of honey, still sweet,
in an ancient tomb.

GHOST POEM

[Don't you remember, you promised to haunt?]
I decide to go to you, in the afterlife, at Pig Beach.
I'm not yet finished with our volcano planet; this is
only a day trip. When I don't see you on the sand,
I know you must spend your cloud-hours unanchored,
on a salt wave. What I do not expect is for your boat
to be made of alligator skin. A leather bed to rest on,
a sun bath. I'm surprised you're alone. I thought you'd be
with your father. Or your best friend. *They're here!* you shout,
They're fishing! Voice glides across water like an ice skate.
In this blurry place, fishing is different. The two men swim
on each side of you—father left, friend right—as schools
of goldfish chase them. Everywhere else, an assortment
of pigs. Pink, dalmatian, tree-trunk brown. They float easy,
fleshy islands. They don't need any thing, any more.

PART III
I LOVE THIS BOAT

High-Definition Microphone Life

If you ever have the chance to sing or speak
or even just breathe into a high-definition
microphone, you'll find out what I found out:
that even the things in life we thought
were soundless, in fact, have a voice.
When the forefinger and the thumb brush
against one another, or the tongue gently
stirs in the mouth. When a lock of hair falls
from your ear to your chin. These things
that you thought were as quiet and soft
as cheese actually make clicks and shhhs
and wooshes that we never listen to.
How reckless I've been for the almost
nine thousand hours of every year
I've been alive to go about my days
ignoring all these luscious noises.
Especially when I know that at any
moment an earthquake could come
and shake or swallow my whole beautiful
life. Then, I think about the people I love,
how all this time I thought I was paying
attention to them just because I answer
when they speak to me, or because
I turn to check on them when they sneeze
or stub their toe—but really, now I see,
how I have wasted my time on this planet
because I never really knew the sound of their
upper lip laying itself onto their lower lip,
never memorized the rub of their neck
against their t-shirt. Maybe their eyelashes
are making a music I can hum to myself
as a way to remember them when they
leave me. Perhaps there is a whisper
when they uncross their legs or a low
rumble when they swallow that would
break me apart in ten places, move me
enough to write a poem about their rattle.
And now that I know this, will the anxiety
of wanting to catch up on all that I've missed

madden me? Make me lose sleep? Maybe
that would be best, because I could lay awake
and spend the night listening to the blessings
in the walls, the blessings in the blankets.
Maybe I will be able to hear my own body
resounding—my ribs tossing and turning,
organs I don't even know I have barking
or trumpeting. Maybe I will hear a roach
sliding its skinny leg along its lover's
backside and then I will know the sound
of a kind of love-making I never even
realized was happening each night
only inches away from my reverberating
breath.

MY DEAF FATHER LOVES TO HEAR MY VOICE

the way we all love best the thing we cannot have. I broke
and re-broke the same toes again and again; and now, they will
never grow straight. I do not regret my first wedding, because
my father, my twin, was arm-candy on that aisle, and nothing
is more delicate than my son's sleepy eyes each purple morning.
These days, my father's hearing aids are small robotic worms:
they crawl into his ears like secrets, but still, he plays car music
loud as an airport; still, the TV roars like a highway; and his ears
don't work, but his biceps are so strong that he arm-wrestled
a glass-eater and beat him in less than a second. Candles, never
allowed in our house, because twice my father watched every
thing he ever owned morph into nothing, into smoke;
his toenails are crooked as mine, but he doesn't care; and I
never worried that he wouldn't hear me having a nightmare
one-hundred miles away because there are vibrations that cut
deeper than all the structures of the human body, that push water
higher, then lower, on land, that make sure there is a very small
little bit of noise left, even after the rest of it has run dry.

THANK YOU FOR YOUR HEART THAT IS ALSO A SHIP.

Thank you for your kiss that is also a spoon.
Thank you for your tongue that is also a planet.
Thank you for your skin that is also gold.

Thank you for your lies that are also horses.
Thank you for your teeth that are also horses.
Thank you for your mistakes that are also horses.

Thank you for your pride that is also a fox.
Thank you for your kindness that is also a soldier.
Thank you for your patience that is also fresh cake.

Thank you for your songs that are also statues.
Thank you for your throat that is also a prayer.
Thank you for your hunger that is also a church.

Closer: A Love Story

"A Vietnamese man dug up his wife's corpse and slept beside it for five years."
—New York Daily News, November 28, 2009

When Le Van's wife died, he knew
the nights would be the hardest.
He liked to sleep with his nose
notched behind her left ear,
his arms hugged tight around
the soft cage of her torso.

On the third night, he couldn't stand
the empty bed for one second longer.
He left his seven children home alone,
walked to her grave, got down onto the dirt

and curled himself into the letter C.
He lay there til sunrise, dreamt
of a quiet river, a river she loved.
For two years he did this: snuck out
when the moon was brightest, happy
to rest only six feet away from her.

But after time, he wanted her closer.
He threw a steel shovel over his shoulder,
cut a tunnel into the ground, got onto
his hands and knees and crawled to her,
to press his ribs against the cold box.

His eldest son grew worried;
asked, politely, for his father
to spend his nights at home.
So, Le Van cracked the box open like a nut,
pulled what was left of her
out of the ground like a root vegetable.

When he carried her back to the house
and put her down on the kitchen floor
he barely recognized her. So he covered her,
head to toe, in clay; spent the whole rainy season
molding her back into the woman he remembered.

Then he buttoned her into her favorite dress.
Put a bar of the soap she used in the breast pocket,
and tucked her into his bed, inside
his long arms, where she belonged.

Five years later, a police officer
climbed-in through an open window.
The neighbors are afraid of you,
the officer told him. *I'm not like normal people,*
Le Van said, *I just do things differently.*

LE VAN'S WIFE RETURNS AS A RED BIRD TO THANK HIM FOR HIS LOVE

"A Vietnamese man [Le Van] dug up his wife's corpse [covered it in clay] and slept beside it for five years."
–New York Daily News, November 28, 2009

Dear My Husband,
I never knew you were an artist.
The statue you made of me was so
precise. Right down to my cheekbones.
I'd almost forgotten them myself.
I watched you slide your clay-covered
hands along each angle of my body
as if it was a doorframe in the dark.
You kept your eyes tight-closed
oysters, trying to remember every
inch of me. Is that where I live
the brightest? In the blackest part
of your head? The place that happens
when you turn off day's bright
lights and all the world's radiant
colors? Is that why nighttime
was when you longed for me most?
But, my husband, we are Buddhists,
you know that skeleton was only
a temporary address, that I slipped
out of my skin like a swimsuit
seven years ago. At first, I thought
of pecking at your ear to say:
Stop this, stop this right now.
I was certain it must be unholy
to love a body with such obsession.
But then, I changed my mind.
I don't want to stop you, I want
to thank you for loving the whole
flesh and bones of me with abandon.
Look at me now: belly like a plum,
feet like spiders, and this mesh
of elaborate red feathers for arms.
Sure, I can fly. But I never wanted to fly.

All I wanted was the breath
and tendon of you, the silvery
voices of our children in the rooms
of our home. Thank you for loving me
hard, for refusing to let me become
invisible.

The Poet and the Terrorist

She said:	What did you think of my poems?
He said:	You know what words like that make me want to do?
She said:	What?
He said:	Untie the machine gun that's strapped to my leg. And sell it, like an old car, for parts.
She said:	What would you buy with the money?
He said:	A tent for us to live in. And a Ferrari.
She said:	What color Ferrari?
He said:	Bright blue.
She said:	Where would we drive it to?
He said:	To get a tattoo.
She said:	What kind of tattoo?
He said:	One that covers my whole face. And your whole face, too.
She said:	We won't be able to recognize each other.
He said:	We can pretend we never met.
She said:	And meet again?
He said:	Yes. We'll start over like strangers. And fall in love. Then, one day, when you show me a photo of the old you, I'll say: That girl, is as beautiful as the moon.
She said:	And what will you do if, when you say that, I become terribly jealous?
He said:	I'll tell you: Don't worry. You have her eyes.

Afraid to be Buried

I said:	Where's the dog?
She said:	Hiding. He's embarrassed about dying.
I said:	Did you tell him he should come out? That it's OK? That you forgive him?
She said:	No. Because I don't.
I said:	Don't be that way.
She said:	I don't know any other way to be.
I said:	Stand inside a door frame—like people who are waiting for earthquakes do. It'll make you feel better.
She said:	I tried that. It didn't.
I said:	Eat some cherries. They're delicious.
She said:	I'm afraid I might swallow one whole.
I said:	Don't be afraid of sweet stuff.
She said:	Can I ask you something?
I said:	Sure. Just close your eyes as you do it.
She said:	(eyes closed) What do you think it looks like, underground?
I said:	Like clay. Fresh, fresh clay.

DECEMBER

There is a girl named December
who works as a hairdresser's assistant
on the Upper East Side. She wears black
lipstick, and has strong fingers. She gives
the best shampoo in all of Manhattan.

Middle-aged women love her, because
she doesn't make them feel awkward
about the tiny facelift scars that have formed
ridges around their ears. December lives
in a four-floor walkup, one-room apartment
by herself, except for her six-foot python.

As she massages avocado balm into the tender
scalps of New York City's fanciest ladies,
she tells them how her snake just turned
eight. She winks, like a loyal housewife,
when she says: "I've raised him since he was born.
Eight whole years we've been together."

She explains to them how she can't bear
to keep him in a tank, how he has the run
of their home, just like a dog would, and how
he sleeps in her bed each night,
in a tight coil at her ankles.

But lately, December sighs, "He's been acting strange.
He's refused to eat for weeks. He turns his head
in disinterest at the plump rats I bring him for dinner.
Pretends as if he cannot even smell their fur."

"And the most unusual thing:
in the deepest part of night,
he unwinds his body and stretches out
alongside me in the bed,
as if he were a man."

[She took him to a Herp Vet in Staten Island.
She had to take a boat to get there].

"And would you believe
what that fool for a snake doctor
tried to tell me?"

"He said my snake has been starving himself,
to prepare for a big meal.
He said when he reaches his body long and straight,
to match the whole length of me on the mattress,
it's because he's measuring me.
He said he's planning to eat me.
That the only option is to put him to sleep immediately."

December wraps warm towels around
the necks of her clients as she tells them
this next part, the most important part, of the story.
"I looked straight at that doctor and said:
          Sir, you really think I would kill
          the very thing I love most?
          I know you are an expert in the workings
          of the internal organs of reptiles. But clearly,
          you know nothing about the heart of a woman."

[She carried her snake all the way home,
from one island to another. He was heavier
than ever that night. She carried him up
four flights of stairs. They fell asleep
right away, twisted together like ivy.]

Back at the salon, the women waiting
to have their hair washed shook
their heads left and right in despair.
The eldest one said:
"December, you are young,
you have not yet learned
how love can ruin you.
You are so naïve
you can't believe
that the very thing
you sleep with
could swallow you."

Hands

What if our hands came first?
What if they were the first thing
that grew on us, and then,
we used them to build
all the other parts? What if
we were allowed to mold
ourselves, with our own fingers,
into exactly what we wanted
to be? What if we could
tell the world: *I made myself.*
There is no one else to blame
but me.

A Horror Story

America is the land of pizza delivery, and Brooklyn
has the best pizza. A girl comes home drunk,
orders an Artichoke Pizza, extra-large, and before
it arrives she falls asleep in her jeans. The delivery man
presses a silver button, a shiny dime, ten times before
he gives up. He leaves her pizza on the brownstone stoop
and rides his bike north into the night. On the third floor,
the girl is comatose, dreaming of lattes and love stories.
A mischief of rats scurry out of their dark tent-like spaces
and make their way onto this scene's stage in ballerina rows.
The aroma of melted cheese magnets their bodies to the box.
Claws tear-apart cardboard; the rodents nose-dive into the pie
as if it were a swimming pool. They fill their throats
with this hot, gooey, forgotten meal, until there is no
room left for breath. The landlady wakes up and peeks out
of her first-floor bedroom window. She watches this moonlit
feast, teeth gnashing at crust, tails slapping the concrete.
She stares in silent horror. She is mortified by their ferocious
hunger. Repulsed by their will to fight for their own survival.
This is extra food, that someone was too tired to eat. They are
devouring it like children imprisoned on occupied land.
She watches the rats through her rectangle lens. Same shape
as a TV screen. She cannot stand to look for another second.
She pulls the cord of her blackout blinds, and goes back to bed.

Not A Beautiful Poem
for Hsiao Hui

I have a friend who is more beautiful than you.
More beautiful than me.
More beautiful than anyone.

But this is not a beautiful poem.
Do not expect to carry a beautiful feeling in your
chest after this poem ends.
Do not read this poem on the days of your life where you feel dizzy
over the gooey beautifulness that drips over this giant world.
On those days, forget you ever read this poem.

My beautiful friend has been sick for three years.
She rarely complains, even though
she cannot go outside for months at a time.
She always says *Thank you* and *I love you* when I visit.
When I bring her apples. When I refill her humidifier
that is shaped like a frog.
She is sick everywhere except for her face.
It has never blemished or aged.

I hear her chant, in a language I don't understand, in the bedroom.
I am in the living room, sewing lace trim
onto my wedding dress
for a wedding that she will be too sick to attend.

New York City is making her sicker. By the time I am married,
she will have left for Mexico
to find a miracle medicine-man in the jungle,
or she will be on an island in Southeast Asia
searching for sun and salt that will help her heal.

When she begins to feel better, she tells me she wants to swim.
I am wary of the ocean. I beg her not to go too deep.
Sea creatures are treacherous, I tell her.
She tells me not to worry and sends photos
of her, underwater, swimming with jellyfish.

Their bodies are bright mushrooms,
small umbrellas that glide along her belly.

When she comes up for air, bad news is waiting for her.
Her sister's body has been found dead.
She must stop swimming and rush home for the prayer service
that will send her sister's soul into the next incarnate.

In the next life, they wish many things for her:
Better Luck, Bigger Cars, Fancier Handbags, No Gang of Men
To Rape Her in a Park, No Man's Hands on Her Throat,
No Jungle Rocks for Pillow, No Dirt for Bed.

My friend wants to go back down
to the soft, aquamarine world, and stay there.
Underwater is velvet.
What do we need wind for?

She begins to grow gills, to prepare for her next dive.
The world of breath and tall trees has brought nothing but illness.
Give me sharks. Razorfish. Better than men. Better than being sick.

I am nearly an entire planet away from her.
I cannot reach her, even if I carve a hole.
I want to have a healthy heart, to give up elevators
and always take the stairs.
But I don't think it's a good idea
to take my chances with stairwells anymore.

She told me the men had knives. That they cut her sister
in places that make no sense.
At the same time, a bloom of jellyfish surrounded her.
She could see through their skin.
They had pale yellow, transparent bodies.
She held one in her hand. No sting.

FORGIVENESS

I am climbing back onto a ship that I know
has a very good chance of sinking.
It has sunk before. I have proof.

But I cannot help it. I love this boat.
I love to lay on its deck, to see
sunset and sunrise from its railing,
to sleep with its plaster floor rocking
against my chest like a body.

I will probably point it toward China,
sail it out into the deepest part of the sea,
even though I know there are holes
in its bottom, no life jackets on board,
the certainty of sharks.

I will just hope, with everything in me,
for a miracle.

Perhaps a great and good sea monster
will lift its back up to the boat's deep belly
and nudge it past the hard parts.

Maybe a horse with wings
will soar into the storm, take the mast
in its teeth, and carry us to safety.

Everything else I do in life is practical.
With logical consideration and reasonable
measure. I think I will let my heart have this boat.

To prepare for lightning bolts, I will sleep
with a car tire, wrap my limbs around the rubber
as if it were a man. Perhaps I will even learn
to pray again, if I can dream up which God it is
I can believe in. The God of the moon?
The God of the stars? The God of the wind?

Love Poem at the Apocalypse

On the last sunset of summer, we carry
a meal to the beach. As day wipes itself
from the sky, a fat cloud of flies emerges
in the same fashion as steam in a sauna,
until we are enveloped by a black fog of bugs.

The kids cry, make swatters of their hands. We all twitch,
slap our necks, spit wiry wings from lips. Our nostrils
aren't safe. Our ears, hollow caves for flies to rest in.

We run from the beach and drive home.
But I am changed. I am haunted by flies.

How fragile I am. How silly I was to think
myself strong, just because I can drive
clutch. Because I swam across an entire lake.
This pampered place, where someone sculpted
smooth roads for me, threaded every wall
with electricity, showered the trees
with enough poison to force the wild
animal-ness of Earth to tame itself.
This is the only reason it does not eat me.

When catastrophe comes, in swarms of locusts,
I know the ocean—that I love so desperately—will end us.

If it were the end of the world, would you choose me
to make love to? Would you cup your large hands
to shelter my face from a plague of pests,
so we can kiss and kiss and kiss
as insects devour the rest of us?
When the volcanoes finally take the planet—
oh, let the tsunami come, and let us go out like otters—
asleep on the wet surface of a wave,
paws magneted, bodies tied together
with kelp. We have woven our own
continent. This surf-apocalypse, this land-less
life, where I am bone-handcuffed to you.
We float away, into the end of everything.

Part IV
Come to Life

Six

I don't know if my grandfather remembers
killing his brother. It happened one hundred
years ago, with a pointy-nosed gun. The bullet
slid through the weapon's hummingbird body,
warm in his tiny palms, and into the clay-like
muscle of the newborn sixth child. That was
the baby's name: Six. After baby number six
was pronounced dead, their mother grew
another boy, in her hollow place, just underneath
her still-tender ticking clock. They gave the new baby
the same name: Six. Did they think they could trick
the Gods into believing that the second Six,
was the same as the first, returned home
from a long stay with the Seamstress of Skin,
a Good Witch who knows how to un-bullet a baby?

By the time I meet him, my Grandfather
seems immortal. His breath is a windstorm,
even though his two spongy balloons
have turned iron-black. He wears rifles
on his shoulders as if they are thunderbolts.
Fish in the water bend their backs in surrender
to him. When my son is born, he and my grandfather
are a century apart. On his one-hundredth birthday
he holds my baby. Their coal-eyes match. There is
an entire time machine between them.
Diamonds are buried in those antique hands,
squeezed between the deepest layers of dark carbon.
Diamonds are indestructible. I want to mine them
from his palms. Let them leak out, let us drink them.
This is my son, he is new here.

One Mouse, One Bumble Bee, One Tooth

My Great Aunt Helen
once spent
an entire Saturday
with a dead mouse
in the toe-tip of her shoe.
She slept in the bedroom
next to mine,
and her Saturdays
were workdays, extra-long.
I don't know for sure,
but I think the mouse
must have crawled into her loafer,
to hide from our cat, Christopher.
She must have pushed
her tiny foot hard
into his soft body.
I hope it was sudden death
for the mouse.
When she told my Grandmother
what happened,
my Grandmother said
she once spent
an entire Sunday
with a bumble bee
under her pantyhose,
his needle-stinger
stabbed into her thigh
for all the hours.
At Christmas dinner,
my Grandfather told us
he lost a tooth.
We asked him
when he lost it,
he said, last week.
We asked him
where the tooth
was now; he said,
right here
in my pocket.

People Who Are Afraid to Fly in Airplanes Love Harder

We do not pretend this makes sense:
eating peanuts while suspended inside a cloud?
My wing-less self moving through the blue,
flying higher than birds do?
My body is not bigger than a mountain,
I am not meant to be more than a mountain away
from the dirt floor where the bodies I Love
are eating breakfast, kicking rocks.
You wouldn't share a toothbrush
with your best friend, but you trust a stranger
to pilot two-hundred tons of metal
through a cold kind of air that will make you
breathless if it gets to you; you have handed over
your entire life. You know, you might only
get one. Your whole wild body is being
gambled; *Are you not afraid of this?*
Are you also the kind of person who Loves
silently? Is your mouth a monastery?
Do you never moan? Has a surge of heartache
never gushed out from the burning inside part of you?
Do you sing? Do you scream? Do you know
that my great aunts waited until the casket
was lowered halfway into the rectangle hole
before they threw themselves on top of the box
that held their brother, father, husband.
Their wailing was an unkempt orchestra of noise,
a monster's symphony—*Where did they think
he was going?* Were they afraid he might fly?
They were trying to hold him fast against
the only rock they have ever known
to be home.

World Trade Center Memorial

In fifteen years, I never came back.
How my life has changed since: twenty-one,
wearing satin hair scarves, streamers that waved
in the September heat like Rapunzel's ladder.
Tied into a royal blue apron, I sold soap and perfume
to a gray color-palette of suits.
Of course there were nightmares.
Who walked away from it without nightmares?
The haunting is a slow-motion replay of that day:
all those boxes of flowery soap stacked like bricks,
tumbling down, crashing, slivers of soap covering the floor
like pieces of crayons. The man who came to buy
Lavander Eau Du Toilette for his wife or mistress, then pulled
the elevator lever up eighty-nine floors to his desk—
did he have to jump from his southface window to escape
the flame? The woman who picked up a glass bottle
of *Sweet Almond Oil* for her bathwater—did she drown
in a tide of thick smoke? The man who rolled sticky rice
in seaweed but never smiled, the UPS delivery driver
with kind eyes, the homeless girl who carried her life
on a wheel cart; once the city was wallpapered
with missing posters I looked for each of their faces
in the neverending collage.

Fifteen years later, the entrance to the train station
is a giant metal dove. I walk under its wing
pushing a baby stroller. In the places where two
buildings once stood, are now square holes,
four-sided waterfalls that spill into stone pools.
It's the windy-est day of the year. Blasts of air
pick up spoonfuls of water and spray us—
a tiny wet mist is landing on my son's face.
Each time he feels it, he laughs, loud.
He doesn't know this is a place to remember the dead.
His joy is large as his face is tickled with the cool splash.
He giggles. Louder still. Strangers are starting to turn
our way, to smile. The sky is a solid
color-palette of gray, but his laughter feels like
what it must be to taste the color yellow.

HOW TO DESTROY A BUILDING

While driving to the mountains with my son
we pass a burning car on the highway.
I check his face in the mirror. I don't know if he saw it.

He did. He is silent for another mile, and then,
Mommy? he says, *Do you think they got out in time?*
Yes. I think so. I tell him, *They had four doors*
to escape from. And windows, too.

I have told him how the timeline of my life
has been defined by burning buildings.
How I was conceived because a man fell asleep
holding a glowing cigarette in an old hotel.
He knows this origin story well: how it was fire
that brought me, then him, to life.

When I was twenty-one, I sold soap inside a tower
that was best known for reaching itself like an arm
into the sky over New York City. A tower that had a twin,
until one day, the siblings were replaced with black clouds.

It is 2024. Every day, the internet teaches me how
to destroy a building. Just last week, a restaurant [her bedroom]
[a hospital] is now a toothed structure. Concrete streets are sandboxes.

On a Monday night, I drink tequila with a friend
who helped clean up the fallen towers with his hands.
We whisper when we talk about the news. We remember
how even back then, even when soot swarmed the city,
never were our hearts so sore to want to pitch
red rockets that collapse and desaturate
someone else's enormous animation.
To turn everything electric into grayscale.
Even with that brand new, raw despair
still erupting in our throats, never did we wish
to make children become ash.

Thirty Days

[April 1, 2016] Dear Jacqui,
Today, in a closet-sized room, with two
transducer belts velcro-ed to my belly,
I listened to your heartbeat for an hour.
A machine next to me scratched black ink
onto a roll of paper. It was the script of an alphabet
I've never known. I think you were writing
your first poem—it is April first, after all.
You have no pen. Your hands are wet
with amniotic fluid. You scribble your words
via sonogramic sound wave to the beat
of that pumping muscle inside you—inside me.
I cannot decipher your language yet.
I hope, very soon, you will teach it to me,
and I will teach you mine.

[April 2, 2016] Dear Jacqui,
You will be born into a black and white,
two-dimensional planet. As it bloats,
amplifies, and balloons, I will try to explain
why it hurts sometimes. I will write poems
to keep a record of the good and gold stuff,
and I will also keep track of the days that ache.

[April 3, 2016] Dear Jacqui,
It will take time for me to learn
how to be your mother. I will try
to unlearn the wrong roads, so I don't
drag you down them. There are things
I already know how to do: cook, kiss,
and write poetry. I do not know which rules
I will want you to follow, except for two:
Do not get swept away by a river of stars.
Do not let a tornado of bees into your heart.

[April 4, 2016] Dear Jacqui,
A week after I found out you had taken root in my belly,
I swam across the lake I grew up on. You were the size
of a pea, shaped like the letter C. The water was near-black.
I was fixed on the other shoreline, watching it get slowly
larger and closer. Today you are the size of a melon.
I've only ever seen you on a computer screen, swimming,
just like I was, in black water. Your curled body, a tiny man,
pinwheel spins, when I dream.

[April 5, 2016] Dear Jacqui,
Tonight I can hardly keep my eyes open
long enough to write to you. Wanting you
is exhausting. We have walked at least
one-thousand miles together, so far. We have
eaten at least two-hundred apples. Just now,
your right leg stretched itself out
like a rubber band. I love you already.

[April 6, 2016] Dear Jacqui,
Every route of love I have ever known
has been measured by the events
that took place during its orbit; an anthology
of flashbacks strung together like licorice.
This is the first time my love has no history,
and exists only as what I can hallucinate might be next.
Invisible love, my imagination has carved you
into something wilder than horses,
thunderstorms, fire flowers.

[April 7, 2016] Dear Jacqui,
Because of you, I am never alone. I try to be
extra kind, just in case you are listening.
I treat myself as if I am fine-spun, delicate
as cake. This world is a bully, and you are
a spider-web I have anchored on each
of my hands like a hammock. I am tip-toeing.
Every thing is earthquake.

[April 8, 2016] Dear Jacqui,
Today, I walked to Brooklyn Heights in the rain.
The sky was a dull silver. I passed Henry Street,
my first Brooklyn address, the first landmark
on the treasure map I have been following
to get to you. That year, your father moved
into the home we live in now. It was ten more years
before I found him here. Once I came inside,
he painted the walls red, and together, we started
hunting for you. You are still pad-locked
safe inside me, a giant, undulating ship
that I built, without using hands.

[April 9, 2016] Dear Jacqui,
Last night, in a dream, I got onto the Q train
and every rider wore pale yellow shirts and golden
yellow shoes. The train car looked like butter, and boy,
oh boy, do I love butter. I asked the man next to me
how this happened. He said, today, everyone, everywhere,
was in the mood for Vanilla Cake. I went home to find
your footprints, in deep ink, on the kitchen floor. I panicked
because I didn't even know you'd been born. How could I
have missed it? I stood statue, my mouth a full moon,
gaping in awe at the Egyptian shape of your foot. Each toe
was a perfectly measured step on a staircase of symmetry.
You. My son. Perfect as a pyramid.

[April 10, 2016] Dear Jacqui,
A poet I know grew hair for his mother.
Hers had been falling, like leaves from trees,
and no wig shop had the right recipe. She asked
her son to make more curls for her, the same way
she once made his. When it was long enough,
he shaved his head smooth, and handed her
a bundle of shiny, black gold.

[April 11, 2016] Dear Jacqui,
I baked four loaves of bread today.
I set half a loaf on the table and tucked the rest
in our freezer. This batch should last until
you complete your immigration from belly to breath.
Each time I pull fresh bread from the oven
the hallway of our apartment building
smells like warm pastry for hours. I use the scent
to lure your father home at night. It's an incense
with no smoke, no flame—and yet the aroma
reaches its invisible fingers out into the cool Brooklyn air
and pulls him here. I hope it does the same for you.
I hope when I am worried about where you are,
or about what ways the world outside can hurt you—
I hope you become hypnotized and move,
like a charmed snake, toward the path home,
because you know there is fresh bread here.

[April 12, 2016] Dear Jacqui,
Right now, we share blood, and breath, and food.
But soon, your skeleton will unhitch itself.
We will still be able to sleep together, not quite
as adjoined as we are now, but close. I will still feed you
and dress you. This will only be temporary. You will grow
your own hair and muscles on a body completely detached
from mine, and as you ripen, your brain will wrinkle and fold,
and as it does, it will forget that you ever lived here,
just under my ribcage. But I never will. I never will.

[April 13, 2016] Dear Jacqui,
Last night, I dreamt you slept at the foot of my bed
in a pile of eggshells. The slow crunch sound woke me.
As I lifted you, pearly triangle shells fell, like confetti,
from your shoulders.

[April 14, 2016] Dear Jacqui,
I carry the weight of one hundred elephants
on each of my shoulders, that I am bringing you
to a life where joy might outweigh terror, since
it was myself who plucked you from where you were,
and it is myself who will feed you daily, so that you may grow
too large for the safety of my arms. Will the claws
of this untamed world ever learn to be gentle and fair?
Will I regret that I stole you from the stars
to have you here with me, unsafe,
on this imperfect, unkind planet?

[April 15, 2016] Dear Jacqui,
My Amphibian Son. You breathe water.
When you finally come to light and air,
learning to walk on this ground
will be as unnatural as telling a seahorse
to unlearn the sea. And as you forget one home,
you will cut footsteps into another.
In time, you will run. Then, as if you have never
been there before, I will need to teach you how to swim.

[April 16, 2016] Dear Jacqui,
I took you to Harlem today, to a poetry show at a theater
named after Apollo, the God of Archery, music and dance,
truth and prophecy, healing and diseases, the sun and light.
When I walked onstage, the audience applauded the smooth
pumpkin-shape of you. Backstage, there was another son
of a poet. He asked me why my belly was so big, then slid
his small hand over it, feeling for you. I showed him where
your left foot always sticks out. He said he remembered it,
the inside place. "What was it like?" I asked him.
"There was an airplane in there," he said, "I flew everywhere."

[April 17, 2016] Dear Jacqui,
Today is your due date. I know nature doesn't know
what such things are, and I know you are all nature right now.
You are science and magic and caveman. All animal, with no
calendar, no electricity, nothing but light and dark and wet warmth
and rumble. But out here, I am all computer and clock and counting days.
I am heartbeat machine and measuring tape. I am keeping track of you
like government. Like a banker. There are no governments and no banks
where you come from. I cannot wait to meet you, so untouched
by anything of the invented world. What a bright green you will be.
How fresh.

[April 18, 2016] Dear Jacqui,
Fruit-like flowers are starting to uncurl themselves on the trees.
I watch their petals unfold, and imagine it is what your arms
and legs will do when I see you for the first time in the flesh.

[April 19, 2016] Dear Jacqui,
Last night, I dreamt that you grew two wings
just under your shoulder blades. They were shaped
like orchids, the size of your hands. Not big enough
to use for flying. In the dream, somehow, I knew
they were coming, these wings, four days before
they broke through. They felt like two dumplings
under your skin. I loved the wings just like I loved
the rest of you. I woke up to use the bathroom.
It was dark outside but the birds were already noisy.
How did they know the sun was coming? How will I know
when you are finished growing every last magical part?

[April 20, 2016] Dear Jacqui,
We are in the middle of a meteor shower. Stars are falling
like rain, but the moon is too bright for me to see it.
I am missing out on ten days of wishes, one-thousand chances
to beg the sky for all my heart's desire. If I could, I would move
a mountain to dim the satellite's glow, to spend night
watching the radiant, wishing for you.

[April 21, 2016] Dear Jacqui,
Prince died today. I was standing in the living room
and SPECIAL REPORT scrolled across the TV screen.
I shouted to your father. I said, "Maybe this is why
he is late, he is waiting for the right soul
to reincarnate into. Maybe our son will be Prince."
On my walk home, I heard "Purple Rain" echoing
through the neighborhood, all of South Elliot Street
was closed down for a block party in his honor.
One thousand people were singing the chorus.
TV cameras flashed giant spotlights. I walked you closer
to the crowd because I wanted you to hear such a giant
choir of beauty. Something so gorgeous, so holy,
should certainly pull you into this city. Listen:
Brooklyn is chanting, in his Royal Purple name, for your debut.

[April 22, 2016] Dear Jacqui,
Tonight is a full moon. The moon is a magnet
that pulls at seas, lakes, and rivers, and some say,
in that same way, it will pull at the water that holds you.
I am wishing for a storm to break inside me, for a wave
that will roll you out, like a tiny mer-man come home,
a super-hero from a wet realm, a magic son with hands
soft from saltwater and eyes like flashlight fish.

[April 23, 2016] Dear Jacqui,
For six days now, I have walked to Chinatown,
to climb the carpeted staircase of an acupuncture spa
filled with twinkling chandeliers and small waterfalls.
I am attempting to use these ancient arts to magic you out of me.
The doctor is gentle and moves slow and soft as she tries
to coax you toward the light with tiny needles.
Sometimes you twitch, or stir, and I envision
you getting into position for takeoff,
ready to make a giant leap, to take flight
into a fog that you cannot see past.
You do not know that I will catch you.

[April 24, 2016] Dear Jacqui,
Last night, I dreamt that the moon had broken loose
from its hook and was in danger of falling.
I was afraid it would come crashing onto the street
and splatter like mercury. I have never been scared
of the moon before. I wondered if I could grab
a handful of it. If it would feel like the inside
of a melon. Would I have to dig it out
from under my fingernails? In the dream,
a newscaster on TV said to expect
the consistency of a potato, if you get so lucky
to end up with any little bit of moon
on your windowsill. I stopped being afraid
when he used the word lucky.
Please, my son, come to me.
Come crashing like the falling moon.

[April 25, 2016] Dear Jacqui,
Tonight we ate at a restaurant called *Chez Jacqueline*.
It seemed fitting, for this night, to celebrate at a venue
that wears the same name we have given you
as your very first birthday gift. You will never
meet your namesake. I, too, know her only
from aged photographs, where she looks like
a movie star. But, just the way I have green-housed myself
to make you certain, she did the same for your father.
She made her way here through a labyrinth of islands,
and climbed the east coast, like a ladder, to Brooklyn.
Tomorrow night, if you have not come on your own will,
the doctor says it is time for us to go in and get you.
How lucky I am, that Jacqueline knew how
to navigate three-thousand miles,
to bring you here to me from a land of water.

[April 26, 2016] Dear Jacqui,
I moved through the day today as if
it was an ordinary day, when in fact,
I knew it was a most extraordinary day.
I baked four dozen muffins, and froze them
in small plastic boxes. I took a walk
in a light gray rain, made a pot of soup
with extra greens. Then, I packed a bag
with socks for both me and you,
and like a whole different sort of Cinderella,
I waited for the clock to strike midnight,
then rode uptown along the East River,
watching the bridges and boats glow—
a parade of lights leading to a hospital,
pointing the way, in the dark, to you.

[April 27, 2016] Dear Jacqui,
Today was your birth day. I feel as though,
since the very first day I learned of your existence,
I have been in constant courtship with you,
trying to woo you into this very holiday.
You have not been an easy suitor. However,
exquisite things never come to us painlessly,
without struggle or heartache. I wanted you
to fly into town like mother nature, on a gust
of golden wind; but in the end, we needed science
and medicine to conjure your entrance to this party.
You introduced yourself in the evening, with small,
shiny, walnut ears, and you wore a whole head
of thick black hair, glistening and twirling
like handfuls of dark, wet feathers.

[April 28, 2016] Dear Jacqui,
Today, the nurses told me that your stomach
is only the size of a cherry, and it's my job now
to keep this small fruit full of milk. You lay beside me
in a clear plastic box. It's hard to believe you are real,
that these small limbs were drumming the inside of my skin
just yesterday. I cannot stop tracing the contours of your face,
studying the sculpted bones, touching the clay you are molded of,
wondering what river gave up the mud to make you come
here, to me, to life.

[April 29, 2016] Dear Jacqui,
You came home today. I trimmed the stems
of all the flowers everyone brought for you.
I am overcome with a tired I have never known,
a sore and swollen that is all brand new.
We are moving very slow together, you swing your head
like a pendulum, looking at me, at the mirrors on our walls,
at the crooked tree branches through the glass.
I stare at you steady and can think of nothing
more complicated to say except:
        I am so happy you live here now.

[April 30, 2016] Dear Jacqui,
The weatherman is calling for rain all week.
I have never known a gray sky to seem so bright.
Each thing you do is for the first time; maybe
the sunshine is staying away on purpose
to keep us indoors, to rest in the steam that crawls out
from the heater behind the piano, and the steam
that rises like church incense from the mouth
of the humidifier. Steam makes the ends of your hair
curl into tiny ribbons. Your yawn, your stretch,
is more amazing than an avalanche.
This is all we need for now.
We have the rest of your life
to deal with the world outside.

Acknowledgments

These poems first appeared in the following publications:
BAP Quarterly: "High-Definition Microphone Life"
Courage: Daring Poems for Gutsy Girls: "December"
Cathexis: "Fog"
LiVE! Mag: "First Love," "Two Kinds of Cake," "How Shadows are Made," "Bees," and "Hands."
Mudfish Magazine: "Thank you for your heart that is also a ship."
North American Review: "Not A Beautiful Poem"
Poetry Currency: "Light for You" and "The Pool Was Empty"
Superpresent: "Quantum Entanglement is the Scientific Explanation for Love"
SWWIM: "People Who Are Afraid to Fly in Airplanes Love Harder"
2 River View Magazine: "Making Love to the Grief Body" and "There are No Tattoos in Heaven"
The Bangalore Review: "The Greatest Poem Ever Written"

Special Thanks

To the Write Bloody Publishing Team: Derrick Brown, Haley Hutchinson, Brooklyn LaTouf, Nikki Steele and Sam Rose Preminger. Thank you for choosing this book and bringing it to life.

To My Favorite Poets, Mentors, and Most Beloveds: Dave Johnson, Sharon Mesmer, Rachel McKibbens, Tahani Salah, Dominique Fishback, Jeffrey McDaniel, Sarah Kay, Samantha Thornhill, Dante Basco, Oren Schrijver, Shvona Chung, Janice Arbeeny, Grant Kretchik, Shaun Anthoney, Jazzy Smith, Saharah Sejour, Patrick Guerrier, Katie Cook, Alex Valiente, April Jones, Limei Wang, Victor Wright, Samantha Waite, Corrinne Provost, Amerah AbdelAziz Underwood, Kayland Jordan, Poet Robert White, Dana Catherine, Lady Small, Linda Turley, Kyla Haniff, Annie Miller, My Cousin Carol, My Cousin Fraser, My Chelsea, My Monty, My Brother, My Grandmother, and My Mother.

To the Muses of this Book: Jeffrey Caspar Arbeeny, My Father, Brett Roman Williams, Laura Medico, Casey Shea, Hsiao Hui Tan, Nonno, Baba, My Great Aunt Helen, Bobby Gonzales, Prince Rogers Nelson, Eliel Lucero, Jacqueline Baksh (in Heaven), and my WHOLE heart: Jacqui Andre Fabri-Baksh.

About the Author

Erica Miriam Fabri is a Brooklyn-based poet and the author of two books: *Morphology* (Write Bloody Publishing, 2025) and *Dialect of a Skirt* (Hanging Loose Press, 2010). *Morphology* was the winner of the Jack McCarthy Book Award and *Dialect of a Skirt* was a finalist for the Paterson Poetry Prize and included on the bestseller lists for *Small Press Distribution* and the Poetry Foundation.

Her work has been published in numerous literary journals, magazines, and anthologies and she has worked on projects as a writer, editor, and performance director for *The New York Knicks, Urban Word NYC, HBO, and Nickelodeon Television.* Her poetry has been featured in multi-media formats including the ZAZ Times Square art installation, short film, and television commercial programming.

She has been awarded a writer's residency at the Omega Institute and has been a featured and/or visiting poet and performer for numerous art festivals and outreach programs including drug rehabilitation centers, prisons and hospitals.

She teaches Performance Poetry and Fiction Writing at Pace University. She is also a Freelance Photographer, a New Yorker, and a Mama.

Write Bloody Books

After the Witch Hunt — Megan Falley

Aim for the Head: An Anthology of Zombie Poetry — Rob Sturma, Editor

Allow The Light: The Lost Poems of Jack McCarthy — Jessica Lohafer, Editor

Amulet — Jason Bayani

Any Psalm You Want — Khary Jackson

Atrophy — Jackson Burgess

Birthday Girl with Possum — Brendan Constantine

The Bones Below — Sierra DeMulder

Born in the Year of the Butterfly Knife — Derrick C. Brown

Bouquet of Red Flags — Taylor Mali

Bring Down the Chandeliers — Tara Hardy

Ceremony for the Choking Ghost — Karen Finneyfrock

A Constellation of Half-Lives — Seema Reza

Counting Descent — Clint Smith

Courage: Daring Poems for Gutsy Girls — Karen Finneyfrock,
Mindy Nettifee, & Rachel McKibbens, Editors

Cut to Bloom — Arhm Choi Wild

Dear Future Boyfriend — Cristin O'Keefe Aptowicz

Do Not Bring Him Water — Caitlin Scarano

Don't Smell the Floss — Matty Byloos

Drive Here and Devastate Me — Megan Falley

Drunks and Other Poems of Recovery — Jack McCarthy

The Elephant Engine High Dive Revival — Derrick C. Brown, Editor

Every Little Vanishing — Sheleen McElhinney

Everyone I Love Is a Stranger to Someone — Annelyse Gelman

Everything Is Everything — Cristin O'Keefe Aptowicz

Favorite Daughter — Nancy Huang

The Feather Room — Anis Mojgani

Floating, Brilliant, Gone — Franny Choi

Glitter in the Blood: A Poet's Manifesto for Better, Braver Writing — Mindy Nettifee

Gold That Frames the Mirror — Brandon Melendez